Somebody Call God,
I just got knocked down

**Somebody Call God,
I just got knocked down**

Taminko J. Kelley

CoolBird Marketing, LLC | Consulting. Content. Copy.

Somebody Call God, I just got knocked down
©2017 by Taminko J. Kelley

All rights reserved. No part of this book may be reproduced or transmitted in any form or by any means, electronic or mechanical, including photocopying, recording, or by any information storage and retrieval system without written permission from the Author or Publisher except for the inclusion of brief quotations in a review. For more information and inquiries contact:

CoolBird Marketing, LLC
PO Box 612
Goodwater, AL 35072
Web: www.coolbirdmarketing.com
Email: media@coolbirdmarketing.com

ISBN 978-1542615426
Printed in the United States of America
Library of Congress Cataloging -in- Publication Data
Cover Design by: James E. Roach, II of M & MR Marketing
Manuscript Edited by:
Taminko J. Kelley of CoolBird Marketing, LLC

Unless otherwise identified, all scripture quotations in this publication are taken from the King James Version (KJV) Super Giant Print Reference Bible ©1996. Broadman & Holman Publishers.

I am not ashamed of my testimony.

Jesus has delivered me.

I am forgiven. I am redeemed.

"Remember ye not the former things, neither consider things of old. Behold I will do a new thing; now it shall spring forth; shall ye not know it? I will even make a way in the wilderness, and rivers in the desert."

Isaiah 43:18 – 19 KJV

"And I shall remember all the way which my Lord God led me in the wilderness; To humble me and to prove me; to know what was in my heart; whether I would keep His commandment or not."

Deuteronomy 8:2 KJV

Dedication

Jesus, My Redeemer

Thank you for dying on the cross for my sins and rising on the 3rd day! Thank you for caring enough about me to speak on my behalf on that great day of judgment. This book was written in 2013, but because of my ordered steps, I waited patiently to publish this project.

**Pastor Brian Thomas & Evangelist Shamika Thomas
Paradise Mission Full Gospel Worship Center
Goodwater, AL**

My Spiritual Mom & Dad…Thank you for enduring your knock downs and walking through your fire so that you could help me go thru mine. Thank you for being true to the ministry & because of you both I was introduced to the Holy Ghost which keeps me and guides me. I love you, but I love the Jesus in you more! May all your heart's desire for yourselves, your children, and others be granted in the name of Jesus! I speak perfect blessings over your lives! Amen?

Acknowledgements

To the Late Christine "Sis Chris" McKinney
Goodwater, AL

Thank you for all the rides you gave me to our church, to Sunday School, and to all the other church programs. I remember that day you were walking down 30 Road…I walked up to you to speak and I had tears in my eyes…You grabbed my hand and said "Come on walk with me." We walked down that country road and I began to tell you about my knockdown and you told me "Baby, *God will take you out of a situation that you don't have sense enough to leave on your own.*" And for that I thank you dearly…I pray your entire family is blessed beyond measure in Jesus name. Amen.

To Tara L. Odem
Sylacauga, AL

Thank you for blessing my business with your seed offering three years ago, I didn't forget & I am forever grateful. You believed in my vision when it was only a "said word".
May our God bless you with good measure, pressed down, shaken together, and running over!

**To my very patient and humble husband & 4 children
Goodwater, AL**

To Terrance my husband of 13 years & to our four beautiful, smart, amazing, funny and talented kids: Jermyko RaShaad Wilson; Tahj U'Mei Robbins; McKay Kori Kelley; and Torrance Kazley Kelley for being extremely patient with me and for believing by faith. You have seen the changes, the tears, the good fight of faith, the lack in the natural and the overflow in the spirit. I love you all for believing in every wild idea God graced me to birth. Thank you for believing in me and listening to me when all I began to talk about was JESUS. We struggled, but we continued to trust in Jesus. We prayed and we continue to pray without ceasing. My desire is that you all be used for the glory of God!

**To my Mom, Janice Woodson
Jackson, MS**

I pray God keeps you strong, healthy and always in good spirit! You are so funny and we always get each other's jokes! I love you! You are the most beautiful woman I know. You should have been a news reporter, (and you know why I say that) but instead God made you to be a woman who cares tenderly for the elderly. As a child and teenager growing up, I always thought that you were so mean, but it turned out that you have a heart of gold. Now maybe I can pay your money back. (I know that you are laughing hard right now!)

Love you Mom.

Table of Contents

Foreword	The Recall on Your Life	13
Chapter 1	What is a knock down?	21
Chapter 2	The knock down	39
Chapter 3	Shattered Pieces	48
Chapter 4	The Wilderness: Isolation is Destination	54
Chapter 5	Getting in Position	63
Chapter 6	Lose control…On purpose	75
Chapter 7	The Process	83
Chapter 8	Rebuilt	100
About the Author		107
My Favorite Words		108

Foreword

"The greatest good you can do for another is not just to share your riches, but to reveal to him his own."
-Benjamin Disraeli

This is quite true! I am filthy rich in the spirit and I genuinely desire for you to obtain the same fortune or one even greater! I am passionate about sharing with everyone how the benefits of being delivered by Jesus is the greatest experience! Everyone has issues that at some point will start to bleed out. You may not have a problem with things like marijuana, curse words or worldly lusts to name a few like I did, but one thing is for sure, you are either poor, brokenhearted, held captive by some type of addiction or habit, blind and don't know what your next move should be, mentally bruised and/or physically bruised. Consequently, these common issues declare "a recall" on your life.

Haven't you detected flaws that cause you not to operate properly? Many of us are hurting and instinctively do all that we can to camouflage our wounds until finally, their too big to cover. This is called getting tired. You get tired of holding on...You get tired of being strong...You get tired of being wrong...You get tired of being a fool, and heck you just want to give up! I got tired of all those things. I also got tired of lying to myself saying that this time I am going to be for real about living my life for God.

When you have gotten tired of running around on worldly energy that doesn't give you access to your spiritual inheritance, you are ready to be recalled. When you are constantly doing good deeds instead of deeds God has assigned you to do, then you are ready for your recall. Point being made here is that you don't need to do anything unless it can store up riches for you in the kingdom of heaven. Your heart will generate a message to your mind that says it's time to be fixed. Automatically, your inner self, which is your soul, and spirit will send a fervent signal to heaven, and at that time God can begin the process of your recall. Remember, He doesn't force Himself on anyone, but your circumstances (of which He allows to happen) forces you to return to the maker. The recall on my life showed me how all the internal pieces were not operating properly even though the product looked to be functioning well on the outside. When you think of a product that has been recalled you think about the refund you can get, the newly revised product, or the upgrade. If you have ever upgraded your cellphone, then you know how good it feels to get the better version. That's what it's like to have a recall on your natural life. When God calls you to be "recalled" you get upgraded to a spiritual life. Ahhh…. the spiritual life.

Over the past couple of years, I have come to realize that on your personal journey through life it is inevitable to avoid unexpected twists and turns. I have also learned that if you are willing to face the fact that you are tired and are willing to "give up" complete control over every obstacle whether good or bad, you will have positioned yourself for a mental breakthrough! Essentially, when you lose control on purpose you are telling yourself that you are going to let God be God. I think that we have mental battles because we try to control too many things and too many people. God must be the one to set life lessons in place. Each of us need the opportunity to "receive" Him and the ability to have gained our own precious testimony. We all must build our own testimony. For example, if you are a parent with:

- a child in college
- an adult child straying in the wrong direction or,

If you are:

- a hurting wife
- a hurting husband
- someone who has a loved one with an addiction
- or, if you are the one with the addiction,

releasing all control over the situation is the hardest, but most relevant thing to consider. I know it's easier said than done, but from experience it is much easier to let it go than to wrestle with the thought of how you can or can't fix the problem. As hard as it may seem to step back and let those you love or yourself get "knocked down", it is the best antidote. We have to remove ourselves from the equation because if we don't we will just become another stumbling block and do more harm than good. Sadly, we may even prolong the process! As you continue to read what God has inspired me to share with you, I hope that a willingness to receive His truth enters your heart. When you receive His truth in your heart it is much easier for the message to flow towards your mind.

5 Things you need to know:

1. You have total victory over every battle in your life.
2. Never forget that it is satan's job to be relentless in his efforts to make you focus on everything that is going wrong.
3. Focusing on everything that is wrong in your life instantly makes you feel defeated.
4. If you are not able to find the good amid all the wrong, then you will never win your battle. (P.S. the battle is not yours anyway!!!)
5. As my spiritual parents have taught me, be delivered from the people! You can't continue this journey being concerned about what people are thinking of you!

I tell you, the multitude can be anything like people or even situations. Either way, the battle is not ours to deal with no matter how the enemy tries to persuade us to focus on the issue. Let me put it this way, if I had of focused on all my own circumstances this book would have never been written. I had to look beyond what I was going through. I had and still have to live by faith and not by sight. Soldier, you're going to need some wisdom and understanding to run this race and to gain it you must read the Word of God. I was delivered from marijuana, hard core rap music, horror movies, curse words, vanity (wanting the spotlight and recognition), and arrogance (to only name a few)! It didn't take months either. Yep, I got tired and got knocked down. I accepted Jesus and received the Holy Ghost. My strong habits were gone away instantaneously. No lie! Revelations from God and private teachings from Jesus during my wilderness encounter helped me and I certainly hope that my brokenness helps you organize your shattered pieces.

-Taminko J. Kelley

"And he said, hearken ye, all Judah, and ye inhabitants of Jerusalem, and thou King Jehoshaphat, thus saith the Lord unto you, be not afraid nor dismayed by reason of this great multitude; for the battle is not yours, but God's."

2nd Chronicles 20:15

KJV

Somebody Call God... I Just Got knocked down

12/14/17

Chapter 1

What's a "knock down"?

A "knock down" can and will come in many different forms like:

The divorce. The possible divorce. The lost job. The Coworker. The position you were qualified for, but they hired somebody else. The job you should have been promoted to, but they asked you to train someone else. The breakup. The disappointment. The fear. The homosexuality. The death. The eviction. The addiction. The repossession. The cheating husband. The cheating wife. The situation you can't control. The pornography. The money. The drugs. The alcohol. The physical abuse. The verbal abuse. The past. The death of a child. The death of a spouse. The death of a loved one. The mental illness. The weight gain. The children. The career. The cancer. The rebellious child. The lies. The humility. The church. The family. The setback. The wrong time. The depression. The boyfriend you can't leave. The girlfriend that won't leave. The lust. The secret. The secrets. And finally, the will you have for your life vs. the will God has for your life…I think you get my point. My knock down wasn't unexpected. I knew it was coming…I just didn't know when it would arrive (you will always know). No one ever wants to fall and be viewed as a failure. Especially if you work hard at obtaining something, it is difficult to let it go.

My story is no different from many… I grew up in Jackson, MS in a neighborhood called Virden Addition which is known as the "hood". It's filled with dilapidated buildings and homes, allies, drugs, teen pregnancy, high crime, and all the ugly things needed to create a hopeless situation. I never had much. I grew up an only child. I met my real father my senior year of high school. I was 17 and pregnant. My stepfather was an alcoholic and is still fighting that demon to this day, but I love him and respect him. However, I remember quite vividly the Christmas of 1981. I was five years old and in Kindergarten. I attended Walton Elementary School and we were having our Christmas holiday program just before the winter break. The next week would be Christmas. The program was over and everyone was getting into their cars to go home. We were waiting on my stepdad to pick us up, but he never arrived. My mom was getting so mad plus it was so cold. We finally got a ride home and when we got out the car she went to unlock the door, but the screen door was locked. She was getting angrier. My mom began knocking on the windows and calling my stepdad's name, but he didn't come to the door. My mom ended up breaking the front window and putting me through it so that I could unlock the door. I remember cutting my leg and bleeding on the rigid glass remaining in the wooden window frame. I also remember when I got inside the apartment stopping to look at how pretty the Christmas tree was with all those colorful lights and glass ornaments on it; All those presents…. "Open the door girl" my mom said. And that's when I looked and saw my stepdad laying across the bed drunk. I finally unlocked the door. It was so cold outside…

really, cold. My mom finally got inside and she went to wake him up to tell him that he had us outside in the cold waiting on him...She kept yelling and shaking him to wake him up. When he did get up they began to argue. And then, I saw my stepdad walk to the closet, get his rifle and aim it at my mom.... she was sitting on the edge of the bed. I began to just look as I stood by the doorway. She had her hands on the long barrel saying "You gone shoot me? Gone shoot me!" Both of their fingers were on the trigger. He pulled the trigger. I saw my stepdad shoot my mom with a rifle. He had shot my mom with a rifle right before my eyes! I was so scared. I remember screaming "you're going to die; you're going to die." But she didn't die. She didn't press charges and he didn't go to jail. After that, nothing changed. The years passed by and I was getting older. He kept on drinking and they kept on fighting. Sometimes with knives, sometimes with the hammer. They fought with anything they could get their hands on... It became my normal. When I was in the 5th grade I spent the night with my teacher and her children. My teacher tried to get custody of me...She told the judge that I was in an unfit environment. Our water was off, our gas was off...But I thought that my mom was doing the best that she could. I mean yea, my teacher had a very nice house. It smelled nice too; like fried chicken, garlic salt, and fabric sheets from a hot dryer. It looked nice too plus the toilet didn't move when you sat on it...She was a very smart and nice lady; but she wasn't my mom. Sometimes, there's just no place like home no matter what the circumstances are- especially if it's your normal. I also remember a significant time when I was in 10th grade. My mom and stepdad were fighting again and this time seemed worse than all the other times. My mom hit my stepdad in the mouth with a wire magazine rack. It split his bottom lip and it almost took it off. Blood was everywhere...all over my English book that was lying on the living room coffee table. He said that he was going to kill her. I thought that she was going to jail and she did too. Yep, like a lot of other people, my childhood was hard yet in the midst of my normal I found laughter. I daydreamed a lot...staring out the window into the sky. Just thinking and thinking.

When I turned 22 I was pregnant by a married man with my 2nd child; he said he was going to divorce her, but he didn't. Funny though, my mother also had me by a married man at the age of 17 in the 11th grade. Except he told her that he wasn't married and she later found out that he lied. History just kept on repeating itself. My mom didn't finish high school and dropped out before her senior year. My mom had 11 siblings. When she was five years old her mom and the 11th child died together during childbirth. The children got split up and lived with relatives. My mom ended up living with her aunt. When my mom had me she told my mom that she wouldn't keep me while she went to school. So, she dropped out. My mom told me that her aunt put me and her out of their house when I was about two years old. At that exact time, my mom's boyfriend whom she had just met was pulling up in front of the house. She said we got in the car with him and stayed...She later married him when I was three years old, and he became my stepdad. So, I never met my grandparents. I really have never experienced that type of love. Again, history just kept repeating itself. Before my second child was born I had already been to jail four times. Twice for being with someone who was shoplifting, once for traveling with someone who had a weapon, and the other one happened while I was working as a sales clerk in a major retail department store. I was changing prices on clothes that I wanted…they finally caught on to what I was doing, questioned me, and had me escorted out the building by the police in handcuffs. I was so embarrassed. And I had already had several abortions. By the time I was 23, I had already experienced quite a few things. God is so merciful, He even spared me then because I never had a criminal record; and charges were always dropped on my behalf. (I am only sharing some of the things that I have gone thru as God allows me to share in hopes that someone might be encouraged!)

I was always a dreamer and as I got older I wanted to look like the women who were professional. You know the ones in suits going in and out of their offices...Going to corporate luncheons for training and business lunches footing the bill. I wanted that look. After having my first child right after high school graduation I got jobs at fast food restaurants and retail stores. And honestly, I got tired of my bosses and other professional people looking at me like I was nothing and talking down on me like I was nothing.

So, I enrolled into college at the age of 25 and continued until I got my MBA in Business Administration. It took a lot of hard work trying to prove to others that I was not just some chic from the hood even though I was just some chic from the hood. However, I ended up getting that "look" that I wanted so badly. I was always a good speaker, reader, and writer so I could talk my way thru some things and out of some things. Now before you go thinking that this is some type of success story about how I overcame poverty, let me be the first to tell you that I was walking straight into a trap.

KEY POINT:

It is very important that you know that rearranging the outer appearance does nothing to the inside. Many will say that if you look good then you will feel good. You may even want all these "things" that will seemingly improve your situation with the hopes of being satisfied, but the truth of the matter is that you will never be satisfied with worldly lusts.

"For what shall it profit a man, if he shall gain the whole world, and lose his own soul?"

Mark 8:36 KJV

"He that loveth silver shall not be satisfied with silver; nor he that loveth abundance with increase: this is also vanity."

Ecclesiastes 5:10 KJV

As we move fast forward and beyond a lot of hurt and pain, after marriage and two more kids later, I had begun to talk and look like those professional women and even began to get good jobs, but I was still that same person. Nothing changed and I bragged about not changing. I didn't want people to think that I thought that I was more or "all that" because I got my MBA. As the years past nothing changed. Each payday when I got off work I would stop by the store and buy a box of cigarillos, a box of Black and Miles, and a bottle of vodka or cognac. I would get a bag of weed, and I would turn my rap music up to the max. Sometimes, I would even reminisce on my past desire to be a female rapper and other times just chill and talk junk…I did this same routine before I met my husband, before I got married and after I got married. Sometimes, I would go to church high, yep at church high. I even went to work high sometimes and nobody ever knew. My excuse for doing this was that I didn't have time to deal with fake, stupid people with attitudes and overrated power roles. I kept visine, gum, and perfume. I was not what you would call a faithful church goer and even when I was younger I went to church just to get out of the house. I was never forced to go to church unless I spent the night over my childhood best friend's house. Her mom made us go to Sunday School. We didn't have to go to church, but we had to go to Sunday School. There was this one time I tried to get serious about church, but I was still fornicating. Still dating a married man. Still smoking weed. Still doing what I wanted. During that time I was trying to get myself together. Even though I was dating that married man I was trying to leave him so I met another guy. He was nice…went to church and he wasn't married. However, he did smoke weed which was our common denominator. His family was Jehovah Witness and I believed a little different…well a lot different. So, one late summer evening we went to the park to talk and smoke. Then out of nowhere these two masked men came up on us. Now, believe it or not, we were talking about church even though we were smoking. So, in the midst of that conversation these two guys tell us to get on the ground. One had a pump and the other had a hand- held gun. At that moment, I could only remember telling my only son that mommy would be right back. The robbers were asking for our things…then the one with the pump took my boyfriend to his car to get his wallet…The other guy stayed with me and began rubbing on me. I thought that he was going to rape me…I began to see my whole life. In that moment, I asked God to forgive me for my sins and I prepared myself to die. And then the robber asked me the strangest thing. He said "Baby-girl what ya'll doing out here this time of night?" I said "Just talking 'bout God…I was telling him 'bout God". By that time the other guy told him let's go…and they drove off with my boyfriend's car, his wallet, and his watch. We waited for a while then we ran and ran. On that night, there was nothing stopping them from killing us; but we were actually talking about God and smoking weed. And God still spared our lives. Even after all that I still didn't turn from my ways. I was too weak. I needed something to help me. I didn't know that I needed the Holy Ghost to keep me and guide me; I mean…. What was that? Sure, I had heard of it but I didn't know what type of power it had…As time kept passing of course I got older. I was not a dedicated church goer more of a now and then type of church goer. I went to church listened to the preacher man and came back home. I didn't think twice about my actions. Can I just be real with you? I was the type of church goer that was affected by the message only when the message was being preached. You know how it is…the message matters to you in the building until you get out the building. I knew to do the right thing, but to tell you the truth…I didn't think that I was doing that bad. I mean I wasn't bothering anybody…I wasn't smoking crack…I felt like I was ok. Just a little weed from God's green earth, hard rap and horror movies…a few parties even a few clubs…what's the harm in that?

Finally, after all those years of doing what I wanted to do… the day came when I got knocked down. What comes to mind is the parable Jesus gave to his disciples about receiving the Word of God. Unfortunately, all those messages or shall I say seeds fell on ground that wasn't ready to receive.

"And when he sowed, some seeds fell by the way side, and the fowls came and devoured them up: Some fell upon stony places, where they had not much earth: and forthwith they sprung up, because they had no deepness of earth: And when the sun was up, they were scorched; and because they had no root, they withered away."

Matthew 13 4:6 KJV

Somebody Call God... I Just Got knocked down

Chapter 2

The Knock Down

By now I'm 36 and the marijuana wasn't doing it for me anymore...I was tired of smoking. I was tired of hiding the scent from my children and tired of going on the porch and around the house to smoke. I had been smoking since I graduated high school. And just for the record...kids aren't stupid...they know what you're doing. I remember lying on my couch crying about bills that I couldn't pay and some other disappointments. I had lost my good paying job. My oldest child was about to go to college and my baby was going to kindergarten. I remember the night of May 8, 2012. I was very angry at my husband. I was in a complete rage! I also remember it storming very badly that night and I was standing in the kitchen alone and I yelled out with all my heart "I'm not satisfied, I'm not satisfied, I'm not satisfied"! Well, the next morning I got up and went to work as usual. However, when I got there I was told to go to the office. I went in and they told me that I was being terminated and to leave the building immediately. They didn't explain anything! I had never been written up and I held a very important position in the company. I could not believe what I was hearing...I was asking questions and they ignored me and told me if they needed to call the police they would...Wait -What?

I couldn't believe what I was hearing! I received a severance package and it was over just like that...May 9, 2012 was when I got knocked down. I was so depressed to the point of just lying on the couch and crying all day. I finally applied for another job. I got it and it was paying more money. The uncanny thing about it is that when they emailed me the offer letter, I signed it and returned it and in turn, they called me and said that they had to decline my acceptance and that they were not going to hire me for the position! I was flabbergasted! I had sunk into an even more depressed state. It was awful. I lost everything. My husband wasn't working and we hit rock bottom. We lost everything accept our clothes, our inherited home, a sectional sofa sleeper coach, a t.v., a refrigerator, stove, and a desk. Things were leaving so fast as if we were having a rummage sale. Everything that I purchased with my own vain glory was gone. Yet, because of my knockdown, my kids had to suffer as well.

There's a story in the Bible of Sarah, Abraham, and Sarah's handmaid named Haggar. In this story, God promises to give Sarah a baby in her days of old. Sarah was not patient in waiting on God's promise and decided to take matters into her own hands. Sarah allowed Abraham to sleep with Haggar her handmaid. Haggar got pregnant and had a son. But that's not going to be our focus. Let's turn our attention to the part about Abraham, Haggar and Ishmael. Now, if you don't know this story, don't worry… just keep reading. Genesis chapter 21 beginning at verse 14 tells us that Abraham arose early in the morning and he took bread and a bottle of water and gave it to Haggar and his son Ishmael just before he sent them on their way. Do you think Haggar knew that this was coming? I mean she knew there were some issues, but I don't think she knew that she and her son were going to have to leave the camp! Haggar had just gotten "knocked down." I mean think about it... She was living in a familiar and comfortable place and suddenly her son's father tells her that she must leave. On top of that, she thought that her son would not receive the inheritance of Abraham. What a knock down! Haggar enjoyed the convenience of knowing that she and her son would be taken cared of if they lived with Abraham and Sarah.

However, Haggar ignored the signs of a great fall. Sarah finally had her own son Isaac. And Sarah noticed how Haggar and Ishmael treated her and Isaac. Sarah needed Abraham to make them leave because of this disrespectful issue. Haggar was about to experience a situation with hardship and heartbreak. Reflecting on the scripture it never says that Haggar became unruly and she never questioned Abraham of his decision to send her away, nor did she tell Abraham to tell Sarah to leave instead of her…Haggar, according to the gospel simply departed.

The bible says that Haggar and Ishmael departed and wandered into the wilderness with the bread and water Abraham gave them. During her circumstance of uncertainty her supply of bread and water had diminished. The bible tells us that she casted her child under a shrub and walked away because she did not want to see the death of her child. Haggar began to cry and Ishmael began to cry…he cried under the shrub and across the way his mother was crying. God heard her voice and even as she cried He heard the voice of Ishmael. God heard them crying then He sent an angel out to Haggar. The angel asked her what aileth her and told her not to fear because God heard the voice of her and her child. He told her to go where her child was, lift him up and hold him in her hand. God said that he would make Ishmael a great nation.

Just as Haggar was knocked down and had to deal with her situation, God stepped right in the picture. Haggar accepted the knock down, gave up all control and fell. Nevertheless, when she fell, she let her situation fall too. The lesson here is that when we get knocked down we need to let our situation fall out of our hand. We fall needing the help of God and the deliverance only Jesus can give, yet we still have a firm grip on our situation. The Bible says that God heard the voice of her child. You see, Haggar's situation was not the fact that Abraham told her to leave the camp. The situation was that she couldn't do anything for her child. Haggar's situation (her child) cried out from under the shrubs on his own. Another point I'm making is that your situation has a voice of its own. Instead of firmly holding on to your situation after a knockdown you should just drop it, bury it under some shrubs and let your situation begin to cry out to the Lord. God sent an angel to tell Haggar that he heard her and heard the voice of her child. God will do the same for us and our situation. He will hear our cry and He will hear the cry of our situation. He will send help and if we receive the help of Jesus, our situation will gain victory! A knock down stings and it hurts. I don't know if it's the disappointment from the person or the substance of the issue that causes us to hurt so badly. And we all know that it doesn't heal overnight. Nevertheless, a good knock down will have you rising from the ground in due time with a powerful testimony or testimonies! When I got knocked down I blamed everybody at that job. I was bitter. I wanted to sue. I wanted to know who voted me out. I just couldn't believe that they let me go. I was so angry! I had no spiritual life when I lost my job. I went to work from sun up to sun down. God allowed me to sit down and review the report. He brought back to my remembrance all the times I slept in on Sundays. I cheated on Him, lied to Him, I robbed Him by not paying my tithes, I used Him, and He showed me how arrogant and selfish that I had been for such a long time. I depended on that job to take care of my family. I depended on me going to work every day. I didn't depend on God. What are you depending on? If you have been knocked down now is the perfect time to realize who your God is…As Sis. Chris told me…he takes us from situations that we don't have sense enough to leave on our own. I didn't spend time with my kids…I didn't even know what their favorite color was…So, what has consumed you and become your idle God?

Chapter 3

Shattered Pieces

12-4-17 Define

"And whosoever shall fall on this stone shall be broken: but on whomsoever it shall fall, it will grind him to powder." *Dust*

-Matthew 21:44 KJV

Fall on Jesus…He is the stone…Don't wait and let Him fall on you…you may be grinded to powder! I think I would rather fall on Him and be broken into pieces than to let Him fall on me and grind me to powder! In the book of Matthew 20: 42 - 44 and Luke 20:13 Jesus tell us about the stone that the builders rejected. He said that the same stone that was rejected became the head of the corner, or the cornerstone. Jesus is the cornerstone…the very foundation that we need. Do you understand the analogy here?

Picture this:

- One large stone.
- Consider that stone to be Jesus.
- Now imagine you falling on top of that stone and shattering to pieces.
- Ok. Now "x" that vision out.
- Now imagine that stone falling on top of you grinding you to powder.

If we bring ourselves to the stone and fall on Him, we can be broken and mended back together because He is the sealant that seals us back together. But if we wait and hold on to our issues and let them weigh us down and never fully let Jesus be the Lord and Savior of our lives then He will fall upon us and we will be grinded to powder. Likewise, often we let our situations fall on us, grind us to powder and then, we waste away in the dust...Vivid enough? Just like when a glass falls on a ceramic tile floor and breaks...and dependent upon the height of the fall, it will often shatter in many pieces and go into many directions. Some big, some teeny tiny and some teensy weensy. Now, if you've ever dropped a glass on a ceramic tile floor you already know that when the glass breaks, fragments are scattered everywhere. You also know that as you begin to gather and sweep the pieces that it's a possibility that you will miss a few scattered teensy weensy pieces. (Of course, I don't have to tell you how bad it hurts if you step on a piece that didn't get swept up!) Well, that is the best way I can explain exactly how it feels when God is breaking you. You will be knocked down and broken in many, many pieces going into many, many directions. It will hurt badly as He reveals to you who you really are…even those hidden teensy, weensy parts of you that you can't see! While lying on the floor immobile and broken you may get stepped on which will result in a lot of people, situations and circumstances being cut by your broken pieces…and this is ok. Once you have been broken your pieces are sharp enough by default to cut anything the enemy lays on you and you must remain "sharp" no matter how small you feel. The Lord will eventually make your broken pieces whole even though you may feel like you are scattered across the floor. However, there is growth in being broken. As I grow daily in spiritual maturity I have come to realize that it benefits me more to stay broken because this is how you grow. If you are having a broken experience, you are in the best place for God to come into your life. He will reveal the most profound and the most beautiful things in their simplest form. Just receive Him.

"Thou therefore endure hardness as a good soldier of Jesus Christ; no man that warreth entangleth himself with the affairs of this life; that he may please him who hath chosen him to be a soldier."

1 Timothy 2: 3 - 4 KJV

Chapter 4

The Wilderness:
Isolation is Destination

12-30-17

"I waited patiently for the LORD and he inclined unto me and he heard my cry."

Psalms 40:1 KJV

"The wilderness is a place where strength is born. It's a place where you discover endurance. It's a place where you become distant to the cares of this world and you are trained to hunt with spiritual weapons. It's a place where you win when you be still."

-Taminko J. Kelley

Isolation is destination...

In my wilderness, I hurt, I cried, and then I died. For more than two years I was without a car. And I haven't worked for anyone in almost four years. And, well I spent all my days in the house crying, praying, reading my bible, looking out the window, going to church, going to bible study, praising God, worshipping Jesus, back at home, crying some more and writing. It was like being put in rehab for worldly withdrawal addictions. No more weed to get me thru. No more rap music to help me cope. No more liquor to relax me. No corporate atmosphere. No professionals. Just me. Just Him. I remember lying on our sofa sleeper literally shaking. I had never felt so low from falling from height. But I told myself that I was going to be for real this time. I was going to go thru the struggle because I had tried everything but Jesus. It was hard... I was always busy and always on the go. When I became isolated from everybody and everything it was extremely hard because by nature I am an extrovert. A crowd pusher, the talker, and the life of the party. As the old cliché says...I didn't meet any strangers. At one point in my life I even had a tag that said "2 BUZY." No, seriously I did. And then suddenly, the only thing you have is quietness, a bible, a pencil and paper...well, you can only imagine. There I was held captive while being captivated by the Word. You are not alone during the wilderness phase, the trinity will be there; God, Jesus and the Holy Spirit. I didn't want to accept this stage because it was so painful. And I have so much compassion for others in this phase because it's hard to realign your thinking pattern. The only way to get thru this phase is to PRAISE! Let's say this: Praise Phase! The more intense my situation got, the more I went to church so that I could be taught the Word of God. I began to learn how to fight my mental battles from the ground with my spiritual weapons. I was being taught by two people who carried the anointing and the Holy Spirit. I needed what they had on the inside of them and they became my spiritual parents, Pastor Brian L. Thomas and Evangelist Shameka Thomas. During this isolation period, I established a habitat for Jesus to dwell. The pain is hurtful and other distractions will come to increase the pain. When you're in the wilderness, the enemy will begin the mind games and if you have not decided to suffocate yourself with the Word of God, he will have fun dancing in your mind and you will be the model child for a mental battle between faith and "right now" reality. I read somewhere that in the wilderness your encounter must be long enough to bring about permanent change, and, that the wilderness can be a place of endless wandering or a place of endless discovery. My experience in the wilderness felt like every door of the world had been locked. I couldn't find an opportunity anywhere. I was still trying to move when I was supposed to be still. This is the time where relationship building starts with the trinity. Once the realization settled in that I should be in the wilderness it was then determined that I might as well make the best out of things. I learned to desire more of Him and to be stronger in Him. I learned that I was vain and selfish.

Everything that was hidden inside of my heart arose to the surface. If you truly desire to be changed during your brokenness God will reveal to you who you really are in the wilderness, and it will really make you sick. The truth about you will present itself in so many ways, so just be ready to get your feelings hurt; but don't take it personal.

When you get "knocked down" it doesn't mean it's time for you to get back up. Since childhood we have been trained to get back up as soon as we fall, but as I got older and roamed around in the wilderness I found that sometimes we must lay under the shrubs like Ishmael, be still and cry out. Jesus said in Matthew 11: 28 "Come unto me all ye that labor and are heavy laden and I will give you rest." What I have found out from experience is that when you are truly tired of something you will stop doing it, or you will do something about it. No one and I mean no one can tell you any different until you have reached this climax. We are always trying to keep ourselves together when we should just go ahead and break so that God can begin the reconstruction.

When you are in the wilderness you will begin to experience life in a new realm. Jesus will rebuild you when you are completely broken, remember He is the sealant! When I got knocked down and surrendered, something like a detox happened. It seemed as if all my habits even the ones from before I got married started to leave my pores. I stopped doing things that had long strongholds over my life. The Holy Spirit came into my life and escorted my bad habits away. But remember, we must die to this unruly flesh daily. As old habits die, other things that you don't know are there will surface. So, always be thankful that God searches your heart and reveals the ugly hidden things. This is because He wants us to repent and live free! Many spiritual things started to happen during this detox phase. On November 4, 2012, I received the Holy Ghost Power while I was praying on my knees in my kitchen and I began speaking in tongues. While you are on the ground broken, go ahead and divorce the world and all her evil doings. Become a widow to the world! You will gain a renewed spirit, a renewed mind, a clean heart and clean hands! Become born again in your wilderness! While you are still, consult with the Lord and as time passes he will become familiar with your voice and you will know His. Suffocate yourself with the Word of God. When you do this, you will learn that your day rests in His plan and not your own. You will later find that favor will be in all your steps when He raises you up again.

Chapter 5

Getting in Position

Getting in position is not hard; it's staying in position that will become your ultimate challenge. It involves discipline, perseverance and spiritual training. Your level of spiritual maturity, your ability to quote scriptures from the bible, or how much you attend church will not exempt you from a knock down. Matter of fact, if you are living, you will be knocked down. Even if you remain humbly broken before the Lord, you will still experience knock downs! Many will begin taking their position in this stage verbally and as soon as the pain arrives they will quickly begin to doubt the promises of God and stray away. If it feels like God is not moving fast enough some give up. When it appears that you have done all the right things and only a few are benefitting from your efforts, the enemy has a way to make you begin to doubt your position. Very few will reside in their designated position because they don't want to get uncomfortable. After I made the concrete decision to lose all control on purpose I found out that for me to sustain my position as a good soldier I needed to be tough enough to endure, yet weak enough to call out to Jesus for help. Simply put- I needed to be equipped. Ephesians 6:11-18 says:

> *"Put on the whole armor of God that ye may be able to stand against the wiles of the devil. For we wrestle not against flesh and blood, but against principalities, against powers, against the rulers of the darkness of this world, against spiritual wickedness in high* places. *Wherefore take unto you the whole armor of God that ye may be able to withstand in the evil day, and having done all, to stand. Stand therefore, having your loins girt about with truth, and having on the breastplate of righteousness; And your feet shod with the preparation of the gospel of peace; Above all, taking the shield of faith, wherewith ye shall be able to*

quench all the fiery darts of the wicked. And take the helmet of salvation, and the sword of the Spirit, which is the Word of God: Praying always with all prayer and supplication in the Spirit, and watching thereunto with all perseverance and supplication for all saints..."

So, don't second guess your ability to endure, just get equipped! The more intense the obstacles coupled with your eagerness to prevail will only bring you closer to the heart of God! How? Because you are going to be seeking His wisdom and asking Him to lead you and to give you revelational knowledge. He will begin to let you know that He knows how faithful you are during your adversity. The reward for your endurance is everlasting life, and the enemy wants you to compromise your eternity by simply giving up prematurely. Galatians 6:9 says *"And let us not be weary in well doing; for in due season we shall reap if we faint not".* Now, will you get tired of standing? Of course, you're human, but endure! Lay down if you must, but faint not and please don't get out of position! When you feel a "give-up" spirit come upon you it's time to begin praising God! If you engulf yourself with the Word of God it will begin to saturate your soul. Have you ever known anyone who went to church and knew the scriptures of the bible, but always seemed like they were depressed, slothful, or always passing judgment and complaining? Well, those people have just gotten out of their position and laid their armor down. Close your natural ears and your natural eyes and then open your spiritual ears and your spiritual eyes to the world and keep your post soldier! I have not compiled words together just to be writing a book with encouraging charm. I am telling you something that I am experiencing!

Look, the more I began to praise God and spend time with Jesus; the more I kept losing tangible things. I remember back in December of 2012 as I was fighting to maintain my position as a Holy Ghost filled soldier on the battlefield. Almost five whole months had passed since my decision to be "seriously sold out" to God. Yet, with four kids and one of them in college, oppositions were coming my way strong and hard! I mean they were coming back to back in an attempt to take me of my post. My electricity was off and a few months prior to that my truck repossessed. It was three weeks before Christmas; my unemployment checks had exhausted; I couldn't find a job; when my husband finally got a job, his salary was less than $25,000 a year; we had no presents under the tree; my son needed a way home from college because school was out for the holidays; and we didn't have any gas money to pick him up. We had just a little food in the refrigerator, the stove went out and we didn't even qualify for food stamps. Sure, I could have lied and gotten them, but I didn't lie. I even had to bomb a ride to Sunday school, bible study and other church events with Sis Chris! Even when I wrote this book I didn't have a job and I just got a car that I didn't have to share with my husband in 2015!

I learned to be content with what I have remaining and to trust in God's promises. The point that I'm making is despite all your hard times, your decision to stay in position must remain concrete. Psalm 34:1 says *"I will bless the Lord at all times: His praise shall continually be in my mouth."* That is just what I did…with tears falling like a running stream, I gave Him praise. I could go on and on about what I didn't have and trust me there is plenty more, so I'll spare you. Instead, I chose to thank God in the mist of my storm. I chose to teach my children about the goodness of the Lord. Remember, the wilderness can be a place of endless discovery! I chose to teach them how sometimes He must test us to see if we are truly faithful and sincere. I needed to teach my children that God must test your heart. One of my favorite scriptures is Deuteronomy 8:2 which says: *"And I shall remember all the way which my Lord God led me in the wilderness; to humble me and to prove me; To know what was in my heart; whether I would keep HIS commandment or not."* You know what, God graced us and that season passed. Living a life in your position takes work and effort. Your decision to stay in position must be so sincere that no matter how intense the pain of your trials and tribulations, you will not become dissuaded to quit or revert to your old habits. Staying in position is not going to be easy. If you are experiencing any type of pain or adversity you should lay this book down and execute a holy dance until you break out in a sweat because God considers you worthy enough to experience a small portion of affliction. Jesus felt pain, and we will too. Even though it hurts us, we should feel elated that we have been chosen for our specific battle. He wouldn't have chosen us to go thru it if he didn't think we could survive the war wounds! While you are in position you will earn a great amount of peace! In Psalm 29:11 it says *"The Lord will give strength unto His people; the Lord will bless His people with peace."* I must admit, having peace in the middle of opposition will grant you a comfortable night of rest! Oh, I almost forgot this important point: Don't get discouraged when you see others being blessed with tangible items. Rejoice with them and be merry! It will even come to the point when you know you are doing all that you are supposed to do and those who appear not to be will be receiving blessings upon blessings upon blessings! But don't get discouraged! God rewards all his children. Have you ever given your child or someone a little surprise even though you knew they didn't deserve it? If you are doing all God has commanded for you to do, then it is not that you are doing something wrong; you just might have a greater anointing over your life! For me it seemed like nothing good was ever going to happen, but all the while God was building His trust in me and I was building my trust in Him. I was His servant and then I became His friend. The pain was where the anointing was…the pain….no one wants the pain but everyone wants the anointing. You can't buy that type of anointing; you earn it during the pressing, the beating, and the shaking while you are standing or lying humbly broken in your position! I think I will execute a holy dance myself after that quick revelation! You see, the Lord is so wise that He will not allow your fruit to come forth before its season…Gosh I love the trinity… God, Jesus and the Holy Spirit! Concluding, here are a few helpful tips to remember as you pray (because you need to know what to pray for) You need to pray for revelational knowledge and understanding because you will need to be able to understand some things immediately. You are going to need the super natural ability and power that makes it possible to know something without any proof or evidence. You will also need a strong sense of discernment so that you can quickly determine good from evil no matter what form or disguise it presents itself in to you. The enemy wants you to get out of your position; he wants you depressed, discouraged and weak! If you are not in your position, then you will not be in a position for God to bless you. You may not believe me or want to accept what I am saying but, "Consider what I say; and the Lord will give the understanding in all things". 2 Timothy 2:7

"Be of good courage, and HE shall strengthen your heart, all ye that hope in the LORD."

Psalm 31:24 KJV

"The disciplined person is the person who can do what needs to be done when it needs to be done."

-Richard Foster

Somebody Call God... I Just Got knocked down

Chapter 6

Lose Control On Purpose

To lose control on purpose you must accept that you are going to do it now and not later. Some of us act as if we have time to accomplish something or to fix something, but the truth is we don't know how much time we have. We tend to act based on what someone else thinks, but as an individual, you must be conditioned and you must learn the difference between life and death. It's 0% mental and 100% spiritual when you are fighting to live for God. While writing this book, I had a lot of things that could have staggered my potential, but I had to lose control…on purpose. God takes the little that you have and multiplies it…

"For when God made promise to Abraham, because he could swear by no greater, he swore by himself, Saying, surely blessing I will bless thee, and multiplying I will multiply thee. And so, after he had patiently endured, he obtained the promise".

Hebrews 6: 13-15 KJV

If it is only an idea, he will multiply it. I only had thoughts, notes, journals and my very old laptop and He multiplied! I remember watching Joel Olsteen one night after wondering about what and how I was going to do something. I had a laundry list of things I desired to accomplish and Joel said to me (yes to me because I took it so personal as if he and I were chatting together) that you have everything you need right now. Did Joel just say that? I couldn't believe that it was the truth. Look, to be something you must see something. There is no way around it losing control is something you must do…Deal with it. But to "deal with it" you must numb yourself to your reality and let your faith fill the gap between you and Jesus. So, you say you only got a little faith? No problem, all you need is a little. As a matter of fact, the size of a mustard seed!

Remember when I said our lights got cut off? It was December 10, 2012. We packed some overnight bags and stayed with my mother-n-law a couple of nights. But I tell you, if I hadn't learned to lose control I would have been an emotional wreck! But, because I was learning who God is and building a relationship with Jesus and had only a little faith at the time, I decided to say to my situation that my physical lights may be shut off in our home, but my spiritual lights are turned on! I was happy just to know that itty bitty piece of comfort because things could have been worst. When GOD tells you to be still…you better do it! I remember physically moving in the wilderness when I should have been still- It felt like my soul had been abducted and had been placed on a "Have you seen this spirit" sign. In the wilderness, it is meant for your soul and spirit to move and to grow. In your wilderness is where Jesus will meet you… that's where He found me…all broken up beyond recognition and there I laid…shattered on Him the sealant. As you go thru your journey I will advise you to revert to a little child that knows how to do nothing. Stay close to Jesus during your crowded situation because you simply can't afford to get out of his sight again. Just be still and do what Jesus instructs you to do!

"The steps of a good man are ordered by the Lord:

Psalms 37:23 KJV

When I was in the wilderness I remember having a cellphone, (one of my church members had paid my bill) and I lost my cell phone for five weeks. My driver's license was suspended because I didn't pay a speeding ticket that I had gotten when I rented a car during tax season. You see what I mean? When God says be still, be still! I wasn't even a good steward of my finances! I wouldn't have gotten that ticket if I had not rented that car. I was only going to the mall to look around. I was sitting in church saved sanctified and filled with the Holy Ghost with a warrant out for my arrest because I wasted the money to pay for the ticket. I got chastened by God for that…

Summer had come and gone and even thru that I remained in love with God and got to know Jesus and who He is to me. The walls of my home were so familiar because I stayed 90% of my time at home. During this time in my life I discovered (and you will too) that the wilderness is a place where you become distant to the cares of this world and it is hard because you are hunting for something with spiritual weapons. You are learning how to fight by doing absolutely nothing and that is the hardest part…to do nothing but pray and be still. Just be still and let God tell you what to do and how to move. You will discover the beauty of your trials and the spirit of God will prepare you…grace is already yours.

Chapter 7

The Process

It's a frustrating experience when mature Christians tell you to hold on…it's a process. I have to admit that at the start of my journey I experienced a lot of those very same emotions. I became very curious and asked God about the process. I was like "God, what's this process thing all about?" God revealed to me my process one day when I was seeking Him. I was seeking Him to reveal to me how to handle and endure my circumstances. God says if any one lacks wisdom let them ask and so I did. I wanted the mystery of my "process" to be revealed…I wanted revelational knowledge. He told me, now I can share it with you! The stages will be strenuous and it will take faith to endure. Some stages may take longer to conquer than other stages…perhaps even a lifetime. Some people may complete the process and need to start over again. I stayed in the preparation stage for months. Regardless of how you are categorized you need to know that it is a relentless aim of spiritual maturity. Once you understand the process then you can have some peace about your position in your process. There is no way and I speak from experience that you will be able to eliminate a step in the process and no one will do any stage in the same order. However, you also need to know that you may be unconsciously in multiple stages at once. Being in multiple stages will cause you to be stripped of things horizontally, vertically, and from within. Nevertheless, continue to praise Him thru the pain and thru the shame. I even sang a song in the church choir and those of you who knew the old me know that I loved rap music…I didn't even know a gospel song or a gospel group! Your willingness to endure these stages will persuade the vice grips of His love to get tighter and tighter for you. Therefore, just as I was in multiple stages at once, overcoming some stages, refusing to complete other stages, failing and spending too much time in some stages I realized that I was not waiting on God, He was waiting on me- Waiting on me to wait for Him in contentment. REAL CONTENTMENT.

As we begin to review the stages of the process, my hope is that you learn something new, or that you are generously refreshed! It may take several days to explore the stages of the process, however please consider the experience.

STAGE 1

Deny yourself, surrender, and receive the gift of The Holy Ghost. They work together one you will not be able to make progression without doing this…However, the Holy Ghost will guide you during the stripping, breaking and isolation. The Holy Ghost is your personal guide thru this thing called "It's a Process." You will not be able to resist temptations or endure strenuous hardship….

Matthew 16: 24 KJV: Then said Jesus unto his disciples, if any man will come after me, let him deny himself, and take up his cross, and follow me.

Romans 12: 1 -2 KJV: I beseech you therefore, brethren, by the mercies of God, that ye present your bodies a living sacrifice, holy, acceptable unto God, which is your reasonable service. And be not conformed to this world: but be ye transformed by the renewing of your mind, that ye may prove what is that good, and acceptable, and perfect, will of God.

Acts Chp 19: 2 KJV: He said unto them, have ye received the Holy Ghost since ye believed…?

STAGE 2

Study the Word & Fasting - You MUST READ THE WORD & STUDY THE WORD!!! If you don't have the WORD in you, you will not be able to fight the enemy. This is your ammunition! Ever shot a gun with no bullets? You are the gun and the WORD of God is your bullet...Load up! Fast periodically...Give up something you love and push back from that table...Make sacrifices!

Joel 2: 12 KJV: Therefore, also now, saith the LORD, turn ye even to me with all your heart, and with fasting, and with weeping, and with mourning:

2nd Timothy 2: 15 KJV: Study to shew thyself approved unto God, a workman that needed not to be ashamed, rightly dividing the Word of truth.

STAGE 3

Elevation & Worship- Know who God is and lift Him up! Even during your pain. Know who Jesus is and accept Him. Worship Him. He's your Lord and Savior!

Psalm 34: 1 KJV: I will bless the LORD at all times: his praise shall continually be in my mouth.

Psalms 86:12 KJV: I will praise thee, O Lord my God, with all my heart: and I will glorify thy name for evermore.

STAGE 4

Pray & Meditate. Simple? Not always. Pray all the time for yourself, for your spiritual leaders, and for others! Meditate on the Word of GOD day and night! Think about His goodness and His many promises!

Joshua 1: 8 KJV: This book of the law shall not depart out of thy mouth; but thou shalt meditate therein day and night, that thou mayest observe to do according to all that is written therein: for then thou shalt make thy way prosperous, and then thou shalt have good success.

1 Thessalonians 5: 16 – 18 KJV: Rejoice evermore. Pray without ceasing. In everything give thanks: for this is the will of God in Christ Jesus concerning you.

STAGE 5

New Growth & Testing- Becoming a mature Christian takes time and experience. It also means that you will be tested to see if you are true…You will be tested by God and by the enemy! If you have faith…Your faith will be tested!

James 1: 2- 4 KJV: My brethren, count it all joy when you fall into various trials, knowing that the testing of your faith produces patience. But let patience have its perfect work, that you may be perfect and complete, lacking nothing.

STAGE 6

Dedication and Obedience- Go to church. Go to Bible Study. Go to Sunday School. Support the ministry. It may seem strenuous, but it is very important that you become dedicated to the mission of God.

1 Samuel 26: 23 KJV: The Lord rewards everyone for their righteousness and faithfulness.

Deuteronomy 6:5 KJV: And thou shalt love they God with all thine heart, and with all thy soul, and with all thy might.

Hebrews 13:17 KJV: Obey them that have rule over you, and submit yourselves: for they watch for your souls, as that they may do it with joy, and not with grief: for that is unprofitable for you.

STAGE 7

Mind Control- What about those thoughts? What are you thinking about all the time? You see... sometimes we want something so bad like a business to prosper, or a career to excel, or even to be married, but soon those thoughts start to engulf you and become superior over GOD. If you are not thinking about him, what are you thinking about? Idle thoughts can become idol thoughts.

Philippians 4:8 KJV: Finally, brethren, whatsoever things are true, whatsoever things are honest, whatsoever things are just, whatsoever things are pure, whatsoever things are lovely, whatsoever things are of good report; if there be any virtue, and if there be any praise, think on these things.

Philippians 2:5 KJV: Let this mind be in you which is also in Christ Jesus.

2 Corinthians 10:5 KJV: Casting down imaginations, and every high thing that exalteth itself against the knowledge of God, and bringing into captivity every thought to the obedience of Christ Jesus.

STAGE 8

Identifiable Conviction- Instant knowledge of sin will come by way of the Holy Spirit. And please don't get offended when the preacher identifies something in you that does not line up with the Word of God. Everybody is not judging you…they just want to see you do well on your journey!

Hebrews 4: 12 KJV: For the Word of God is quick, and powerful, and sharper than any two-edged sword, piercing even to the dividing asunder of soul and spirit, and of the joints and marrow, and is a discerner of the thoughts and intents of the heart.

2 Timothy 4:2 KJV: Preach the Word; be instant in season, out of season; reprove, rebuke, exhort with all long suffering and doctrine.

STAGE 9

Worshipping idol Gods - Beware of those phones, social media, devices, intangibles and tangibles!

Exodus 20:3 KJV: Thou shalt have no other Gods before me.

Jeremiah 1: 16 KJV: I will pronounce my judgments on my people because of their wickedness in forsaking me, in burning incense to other God and in worshiping what their hands have made.

STAGE 10

Conquering Situations: Tenacity should be one of the many things you ask for because it is the quality of being able to grip something firmly. It also means being very determined, continuing to exist, persistence and endurance. And don't confuse this with holding on to your situation. Drop the situation and grip the Word of God firmly! (Remember Stage 1…you need the Holy Ghost!)

Philippians 4:13 KJV: I can do all things thru Christ Jesus who strengthens me.

Romans 8: 37 KJV: Nay, in all things we are more than conquerors through Him that loved us.

STAGE 11

Confrontation- The Face Off: Who you desire to be vs. who God created you to be: Remember...when you are confused this is not God...He is not the author of confusion. Nevertheless, do ask that the will of your life be done according to His purpose...Ask Him for His divine will for your life...and not His permissive will!

Jeremiah 29: 11 KJV: For I know the thoughts that I think toward you, saith the LORD, thoughts of peace, and not of evil, to give you an expected end.

1 Corinthians 14:33 KJV: For God is not the author of confusion, but of peace, as in all churches of the saints.

STAGE 12

Stay Humble. Open your heart, your ears, and SHUT YOUR MOUTH! Stay in a position to learn…remember…this is a process. Just because you have gone thru several stages doesn't mean you have earned your heavenly crowns…You must continue this race until Jesus comes to get us! He will use you in His timing…not yours, so remain HUMBLE!

1 Peter 5:6 KJV: Humble yourselves therefore under the mighty hand of God, that he may exalt you in due time:

James 1:19 KJV: Wherefore, my beloved brethren, let every man be swift to hear, slow to speak, slow to wrath.

Ok…now you have an idea of the process I experienced. It's a perpetual process for believers. I pray you endure to the end and more importantly I pray you receive the Holy Ghost.

Chapter 8

Rebuilt

Dear God:

I have realized that everyone is not or will not be exceedingly excited about the discoveries of your presence and mercy and I pray they will get there; But as for me and my house I am beyond excited! My heart is overflowed with joy and my soul is like a new home filled with the finest furniture that you have chosen and that Jesus gave opinion on where everything should be placed! I have never felt this rare feeling, ever! To love someone I never seen; to believe in a Word I never knew. Jesus, you are so marvelous! God, you allowed Him to die and rise on the third day, but you allowed me to die and rise on the same day! You made the Word flesh and because of this I AM REBUILT!

Amen

The next minute in life is a new beginning. After you have been knocked down and are traveling within your particular stage of the process, you are entering a new beginning! When God has rebuilt you, or recalled you, He will restore all the lost and wasted time. Just like the Israelites who were away from their home a long time we are also away from our home when we are not in fellowship with Jesus. When the Israelites returned to Jerusalem they needed to rebuild their city because the temple was gone. God needed them to rebuild because He needed a place of worship or dwelling. The Israelites were afraid to rebuild, but they did it anyway. They faced their fear and trusted God. Our bodies need to be rebuilt daily because we must die to this flesh daily. Our temple or our body must remain in a position where the Holy Spirit can stay. And trust me, its hard work! God desires for his Holy Spirit to dwell in us and for this to happen, we cannot be afraid to let Jesus come in and rebuild our brokenness after a dreadful knock down. When the Israelites rebuilt their city, they were excited- they sang songs and played instruments. Therefore, when we have been rebuilt, our city or our body, should sing and dance! We must thank God in our actions and not by our Words for giving us His precious mercy and grace. When you have been rebuilt you will understand the realization of everything you had to endure. Sometimes our prayers and heart's desires are being provided to us and we don't even realize it because we have asked God for so many things. In Psalms 37:4 it says "Delight yourself in Him and He will give you the desires of your heart..." Sometimes the desires of our hearts are things we never ask Him. When I was working in the corporate world I worked from sun up to literally sun down trying to make certain that I was on top of my game. I was always away from my kids. As I said before, I didn't know their favorite color. I had bought a new stove and hadn't even cooked on it much! It still looked brand new...My kids would say momma doesn't cook anymore and I would just laugh not realizing that I was blind. My children were growing in front of me and I didn't see them...and they didn't see me. I would also think about how I didn't spend time with my two older sons. I had them young and I just wanted to party and hang out with my friends. Well, I was repeating the same thing with my two younger children. The only difference was that I traded my club friends for corporate associates and assignments. While getting older and still not mature, I began slowing down thinking of the neglect. I didn't ask God to restore those years, but He did it anyway. He took me off my job after I confessed that I wasn't satisfied! The years I spent unemployed and literally being still and isolated was a time that was given back. I learned their favorite colors, their personalities, we did projects and I even used that stove...I used it so much that the cord burned out and we needed a new stove. I never baked so many cookies...I learned who I was created to be a praise warrior, a prayer warrior, a Word chaser and a sojourner of the truth until the day of Jesus Christ. I rediscovered my God given gifts and talents and He even gave me gifts of the spirit! All those stolen years were restored! Praise God! Naturally, it is easy to complain and cry, but God can and will recall, rebuild and restore those damaged years. God wants to give you the desires of your heart and He wants to answer your prayers. After you have been rebuilt you'll notice that you are content and the things you once wanted just doesn't matter anymore. He knows what you really have tucked away in the depths of your heart. He wants to restore what the devil took from you and He wants to rebuild you after your big nasty knock down. You are somebody even during your troubles no matter the situation. Hey…I wrote this book during my knock down.

And I will restore to you the years that the locust hath eaten, the cankerworm, and the caterpillar, and the palmerworm, my great army which I sent among you

Joel 2:25 KJV

About the Author

Taminko J. Kelley is a native of Jackson, Mississippi, but currently resides in Goodwater, AL with her husband Terrance and their four children Jermyko, Tahj, McKay and Kaz. They are members of Paradise Mission Full Gospel Worship Center located in Goodwater, AL where Brian L. Thomas is the Pastor and Evangelist Shameka Thomas is the First Lady. Taminko teaches Youth Sunday School and Youth Bible Study. She is a speaker on the topic of "Faith to Overcome Your Current Situation". She has an MBA in Business Administration, and is a licensed Cosmetologist with the brand name "Vintage Dolls". She is the owner of CoolBird Marketing, LLC, a Business Consulting & Brand Awareness Solutions Agency specializing in: Project Management, Process Improvement, Strategic Planning Content Development, Copywriting, Editing & Proofreading, Voice Over & Videography. Her personal mission statement is "To work with passion and indubitable performance." For additional inquiries or to book Taminko J. Kelley for speaking engagements or workshops Write to:

CoolBird Marketing, LLC, Attn: Taminko J. Kelley, PO Box 612, Goodwater, AL 35072, or Email: Media@coolbirdmarketing.com or visit our website at: www.coolbirdmarketing.com.

My Favorite Words

Accomplish	Expecting	Mountain
Amputate	Faith	Persistent
Commit	Focused	Priority
Consistent	Hind's feet	Routine
Dedicated	Holy Ghost	Rule the Spirit!
Determined	Jesus	Suddenly
Disciplined	Loyal	Time Sensitive
Establish	Master	

Being Confident of this very thing, that he which hath begun a good work in you will perform it until the day of Jesus Christ.

Philippians 1:6 KJV